OF MONSTERS AND MEN

MY HEAD IS AN ANIMAL

ISBN 978-1-4803-5235-3

HAL•LEONARD®
CORPORATION
7777 W. BLUEMOUND RD. P.O. BOX 13819 MILWAUKEE, WI 53213

For all works contained herein:
Unauthorized copying, arranging, adapting, recording, Internet posting, public performance,
or other distribution of the printed music in this publication is an infringement of copyright.
Infringers are liable under the law.

Visit Hal Leonard Online at
www.halleonard.com

DIRTY PAWS

Words and Music by NANNA BRYNDIS HILMARSDOTTIR,
RAGNAR THORHALLSSON and ARNI GUDJONSSON

Copyright © 2011 Sony/ATV Music Publishing LLC
All Rights Administered by Sony/ATV Music Publishing LLC, 8 Music Square West, Nashville, TN 37203
International Copyright Secured   All Rights Reserved

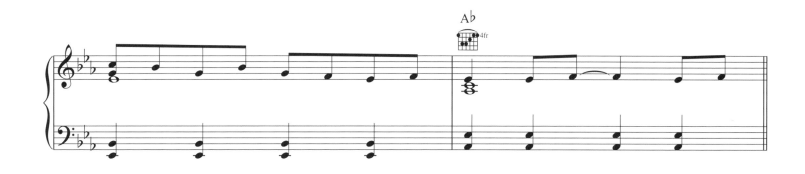

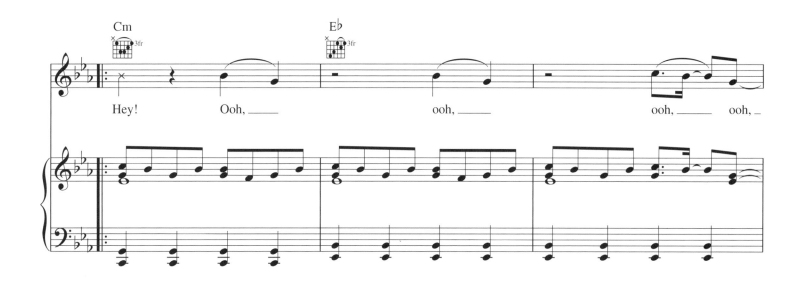

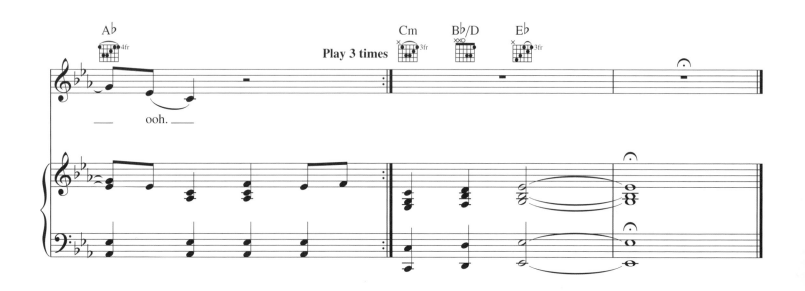

KING AND LIONHEART

Words and Music by NANNA BRYNDIS HILMARSDOTTIR
and RAGNAR THORHALLSSON

Copyright © 2011 Sony/ATV Music Publishing LLC
All Rights Administered by Sony/ATV Music Publishing LLC, 8 Music Square West, Nashville, TN 37203
International Copyright Secured   All Rights Reserved

MOUNTAIN SOUND

Words and Music by NANNA BRYNDIS HILMARSDOTTIR,
RAGNAR THORHALLSSON and ARNAR ROSENKRANZ HILMARSSON

Copyright © 2011 Sony/ATV Music Publishing LLC
All Rights Administered by Sony/ATV Music Publishing LLC, 8 Music Square West, Nashville, TN 37203
International Copyright Secured   All Rights Reserved

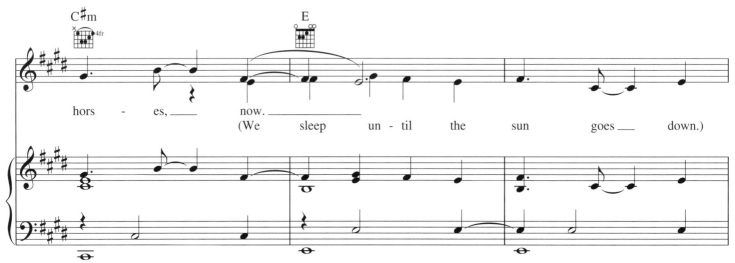

SLOW AND STEADY

Words and Music by NANNA BRYNDIS HILMARSDOTTIR,
RAGNAR THORHALLSSON, KRISTJAN PALL KRISTJANSSON,
ARNAR ROSENKRANZ HILMARSSON, ARNI GUDJONSSON
and BRYNJAR LEIFSSON

The lights go ____ out, ____ I am all a - ____ lone.
My dear old ____ friend, ____ take me for a ____ spin.

All the trees out - side ____ are bur - ied in the
Two wolves in the dark, ____ run - ning in the

Copyright © 2011 Sony/ATV Music Publishing LLC
All Rights Administered by Sony/ATV Music Publishing LLC, 8 Music Square West, Nashville, TN 37203
International Copyright Secured   All Rights Reserved

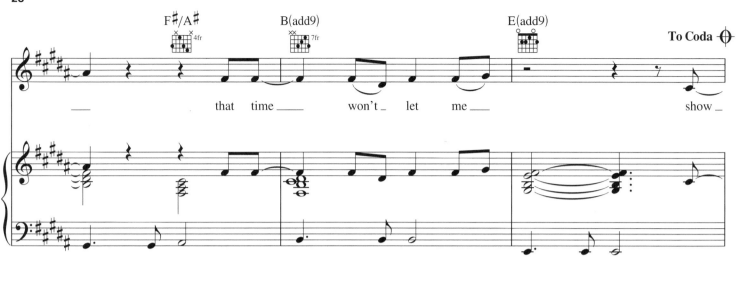

To Coda

that time ____ won't _ let me ____ show _

___ what I want to show. _____

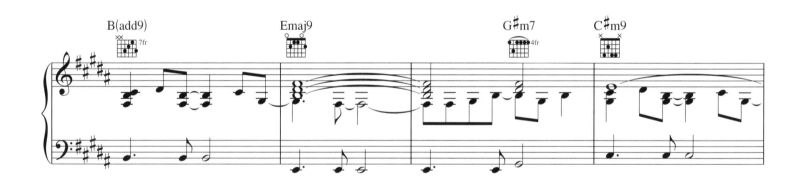

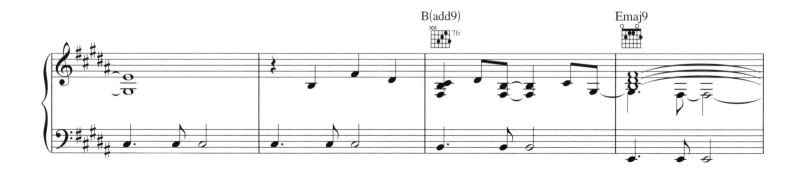

FROM FINNER

Words and Music by NANNA BRYNDIS HILMARSDOTTIR,
RAGNAR THORHALLSSON, ARNAR ROSENKRANZ HILMARSSON,
BRYNJAR LEIFSSON and ARNI GUDJONSSON

Copyright © 2011 Sony/ATV Music Publishing LLC
All Rights Administered by Sony/ATV Music Publishing LLC, 8 Music Square West, Nashville, TN 37203
International Copyright Secured   All Rights Reserved

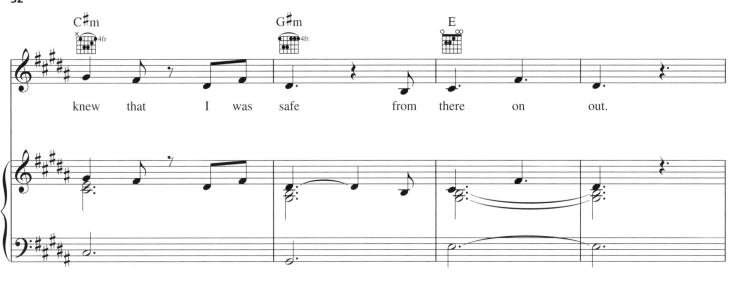

knew that I was safe from there on out.

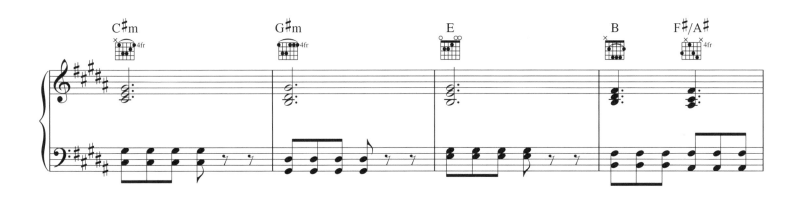

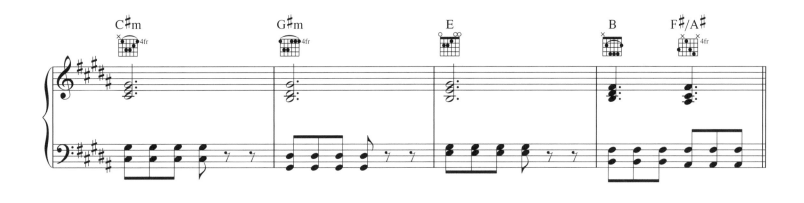

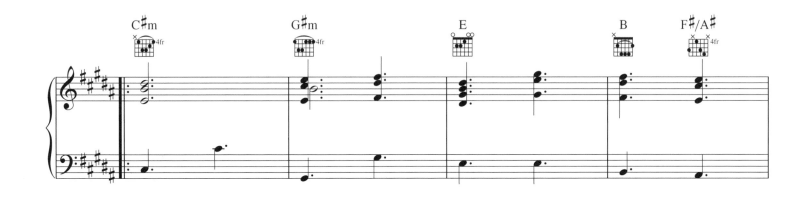

LITTLE TALKS

Words and Music by NANNA BRYNDIS HILMARSDOTTIR
and RAGNAR THORHALLSSON

*Recorded a half step higher.

Copyright © 2011 Sony/ATV Music Publishing LLC
All Rights Administered by Sony/ATV Music Publishing LLC, 8 Music Square West, Nashville, TN 37203
International Copyright Secured   All Rights Reserved

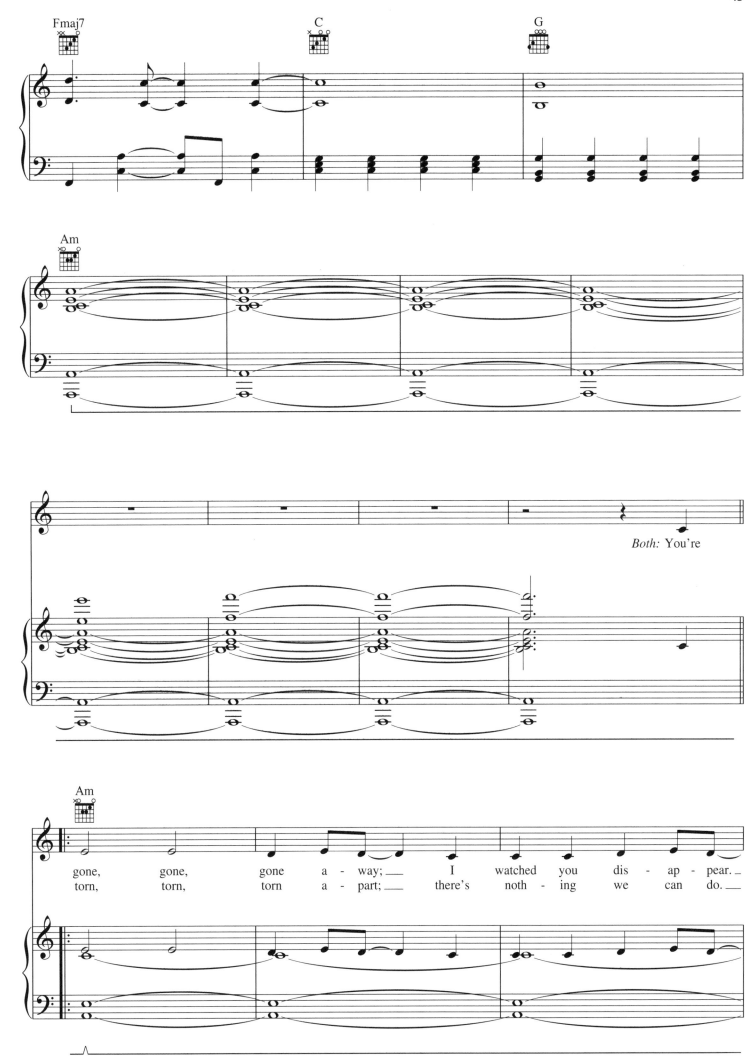

SIX WEEKS

Words and Music by NANNA BRYNDIS HILMARSDOTTIR,
RAGNAR THORHALLSSON and ARNAR ROSENKRANZ HILMARSSON

Copyright © 2011 Sony/ATV Music Publishing LLC
All Rights Administered by Sony/ATV Music Publishing LLC, 8 Music Square West, Nashville, TN 37203
International Copyright Secured   All Rights Reserved

LOVE LOVE LOVE

Words and Music by
NANNA BRYNDIS HILMARSDOTTIR

Copyright © 2011 Sony/ATV Music Publishing LLC
All Rights Administered by Sony/ATV Music Publishing LLC, 8 Music Square West, Nashville, TN 37203
International Copyright Secured   All Rights Reserved

YOUR BONES

Words and Music by NANNA BRYNDIS HILMARSDOTTIR
and RAGNAR THORHALLSSON

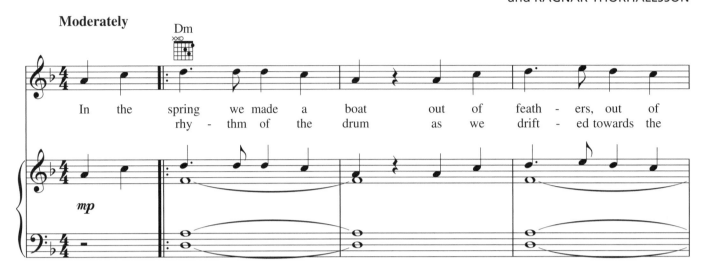

In the spring we made a boat out of feath-ers, out of
rhy-thm of the drum as we drift-ed towards the

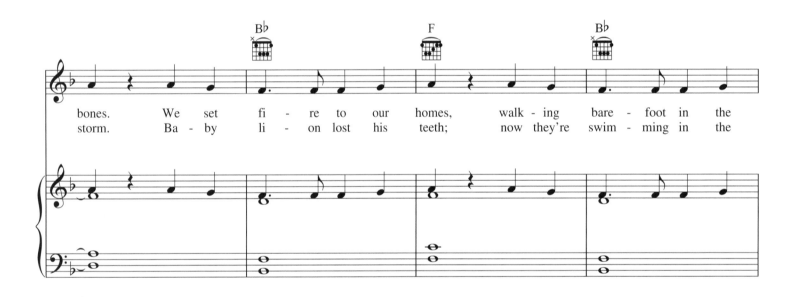

bones. We set fi-re to our homes, walk-ing bare-foot in the
storm. Ba-by li-on lost his teeth; now they're swim-ming in the

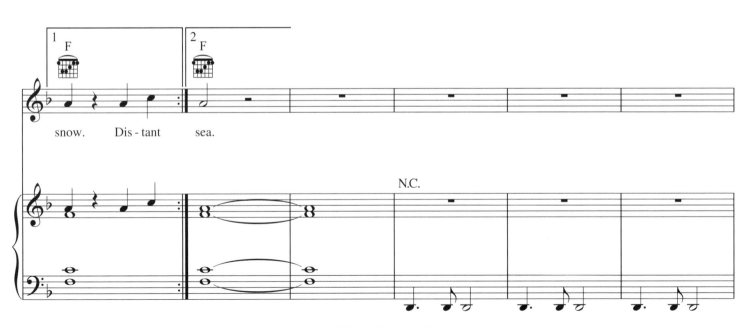

snow. Dis-tant sea.

Copyright © 2011 Sony/ATV Music Publishing LLC
All Rights Administered by Sony/ATV Music Publishing LLC, 8 Music Square West, Nashville, TN 37203
International Copyright Secured   All Rights Reserved

SLOOM

Words and Music by NANNA BRYNDIS HILMARSDOTTIR,
RAGNAR THORHALLSSON and ARNAR ROSENKRANZ HILMARSSON

Pedal ad lib.

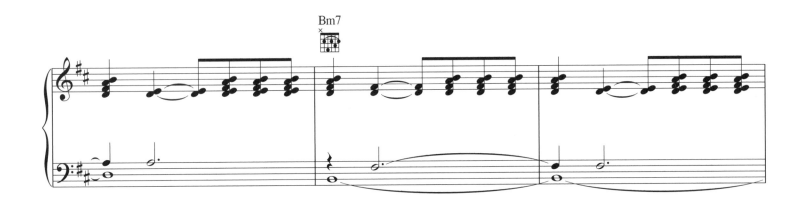

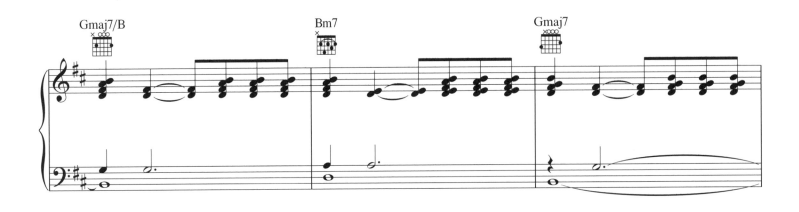

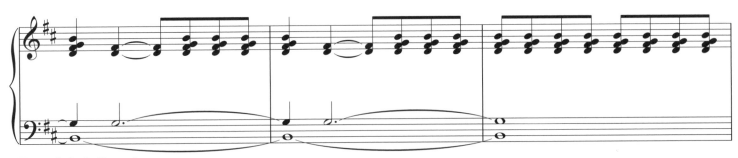

*Recorded a half step lower.

Copyright © 2011 Sony/ATV Music Publishing LLC
All Rights Administered by Sony/ATV Music Publishing LLC, 8 Music Square West, Nashville, TN 37203
International Copyright Secured   All Rights Reserved

broth - er _____ as well.

So

love me moth - er _____

and love me

LAKEHOUSE

Words and Music by NANNA BRYNDIS HILMARSDOTTIR,
RAGNAR THORHALLSSON and BRYNJAR LEIFSSON

Copyright © 2011 Sony/ATV Music Publishing LLC
All Rights Administered by Sony/ATV Music Publishing LLC, 8 Music Square West, Nashville, TN 37203
International Copyright Secured   All Rights Reserved

YELLOW LIGHT

Words and Music by NANNA BRYNDIS HILMARSDOTTIR,
RAGNAR THORHALLSSON and ARNAR ROSENKRANZ HILMARSSON

Copyright © 2011 Sony/ATV Music Publishing LLC
All Rights Administered by Sony/ATV Music Publishing LLC, 8 Music Square West, Nashville, TN 37203
International Copyright Secured   All Rights Reserved